Racer Girls

By Bob Woods

Published in the United States of America by The Child's World®
P.O. Box 326 • Chanhassen, MN 55317-0326
800-599-READ • www.childsworld.com

ACKNOWLEDGMENTS

The Child's World®: Mary Berendes, Publishing Director

Produced by Shoreline Publishing Group LLC
President / Editorial Director: James Buckley, Jr.
Designer: Tom Carling, carlingdesign.com
Cover Art: Slimfilms
Copy Editor: Beth Adelman

Photo Credits
Cover—Getty Images (4).
Interior—AP/Wide World: 24, 26, 28; Corbis: 12; Getty Images: 5, 6, 7, 8, 10, 11, 16, 18, 20, 22.

Copyright © 2007 by The Child's World®
All rights reserved. No part of this book may be reproduced or utilized in any form or by any means without written permission from the publisher.

LIBRARY OF CONGRESS CATALOGING-IN-PUBLICATION DATA

Woods, Bob.
 Racer girls / by Bob Woods.
   p. cm. — (Girls rock!)
 Includes bibliographical references and index.
 ISBN 1-59296-742-6 (library bound : alk. paper)
 1. Women automobile racing drivers—Biography—Juvenile literature. I. Title. II. Series.
 GV1032.A1W672 2006
 796.72092'2—dc22

2006002312

CONTENTS

4 **CHAPTER 1**
Make Room for Danica

12 **CHAPTER 2**
Good Ol' Boys and Girls

22 **CHAPTER 3**
Other Kinds of Racing

30 **GLOSSARY**

31 **FIND OUT MORE**

32 **INDEX**

1

MAKE ROOM FOR Danica

The speedy sport of race car driving isn't just for men! Many great women have taken their place behind the wheel, driving all sorts of race cars.

In 2005, Danica Patrick became perhaps the best-known woman racer. She came in fourth in the 2005 Indianapolis 500. That was the best finish ever for a woman in that 94-year-old race.

Ready to race! Danica showed that women can be just as good as men on the race track with her 2005 success.

Danica is following some great racers. For instance, in 1977, Janet Guthrie made history by becoming the first woman to start NASCAR's Daytona 500.

Danica Patrick was born on March 25, 1982, in Beloit, Wisconsin. She grew up in Roscoe, Illinois. She started racing when she was just 10!

Go-karts are low to the ground. Racers steer them around courses with tight corners.

Danica drove special racing go-karts. Over the next several years, she won dozens of races and several national championships.

By age 16, Danica was ready to race bigger, faster cars. In 2000, she came in second in the Formula Ford Festival in Britain. Danica raced against some great drivers, and her finish was the best any American ever had. Formula Fords are **open-wheel** racers. They are sort of like smaller versions of U.S. Indy cars.

Danica's early success brought her a lot of attention from the media. That's her at the bottom of the picture, looking up from a crowd of reporters.

Here's Danica driving around a curve during her history-making Indy 500 run in 2005.

Danica finally made it up to the Indy Racing League (IRL) in 2005. She became a member of the Rahal Letterman Racing team. Late-night television host David Letterman is one of the team's owners.

On May 29, 2005, Danica started the 89th annual Indianapolis 500 in the number-four position. The other 32 drivers in the field were men. They all raced around the 2½-mile (4-km) oval track for 200 **laps**, at speeds of over 200 miles (322 km) per hour.

On the 57th lap, Danica zoomed into the lead. It was the first time in the history of the Indy 500 that a woman driver led the race. She led for a total of 19 laps on that super Sunday race.

Indy 500 facts:
— A.J. Foyt, Al Unser Sr., and Rick Mears have won the most Indy 500s, with four titles each.
— The very first Indy winner was Ray Harroun, in 1911. His top speed was only 74 miles (119 km) per hour!
— The track was first made of bricks, so the Speedway is nicknamed the "Brickyard."

The leaders of the race kept changing toward the end. With just 10 laps to go, Danica passed the leader and went in front again. The crowd of 300,000 stood and cheered her on!

Danica Data

Favorite foods: fish, veggies, fruit
Favorite singer: Alanis Morissette
Favorite actors: Adam Sandler, Jim Carrey
Favorite music: anything but country and classical
Favorite car: Ferrari 360
Hobbies: working out, in-line skating, traveling
Workouts: running, weight training, extreme yoga
Dog: miniature schnauzer named Billy

Unfortunately, Danica's car was just about out of gas. With four laps to go, Dan Wheldon passed her and went on to take the **checkered flag**. Danica finished fourth— only 4.5 seconds behind— and was voted Rookie of the Year! She raced in 16 other IRL events that season.

Once she puts on her safety helmet, Danica is just another driver trying to win the race.

Reporters always ask Danica what it's like to compete against men. "Hey, I'm just a racer who happens to be a woman," she says.

2

GOOD OL' BOYS and Girls

Stock car racing is different from Indy car racing. Indy cars have long, narrow bodies, and the wheels aren't covered. Stock cars look more like the cars you see people driving on the street. Inside, though, stock cars are specially built for racing. They don't have windows, headlights, heat, air conditioning, or even a radio. They do have big, powerful engines, though.

NASCAR started in the South in the late 1940s. Back then, daredevil drivers—often called "good ol' boys"—raced their cars around oval dirt tracks. As the sport became more and more popular, NASCAR built huge paved tracks in cities all across the country.

NASCAR stands for the National Association for Stock Car Auto Racing.

Early stock car races were held on dirt tracks, leading to dusty rides like this one.

Funny fact: Ethel's brother Tim sometimes drove in races with a monkey named Jocko Flocko in the car with him!

Early stock car racing stars included men like Lee Petty, Junior Johnson, Ralph Earnhardt, Fireball Roberts, and the Flock Brothers—Bob, Fonty, and Tim. The Flock's sister, Ethel, caught the racing bug, too. Ethel (named after a type of gasoline) raced in more than a hundred events. On July 10, 1949, she joined her brothers for a NASCAR race. She finished 11th—ahead of Bob and Fonty.

Sara Christian was another female racing pioneer. She

competed in six NASCAR events in 1949, finishing one race in fifth place. Louise Smith was in 11 NASCAR races from 1949 to 1952.

Louise Smith is in the International Motor Sports Hall of Fame.

Shawna Robinson has raced in just about anything that can go fast!

Today, there are dozens of local stock car races every weekend around the country. More and more young women are taking part in them. Several women have made it up to NASCAR's three major series: Nextel Cup, Busch Grand National, and Craftsman Truck.

Patty Moise started her first Busch race in 1986. Over the next 12 years, she raced in 132 more. From 1987 to 1989, she was in five races at the top level, the Nextel Cup.

Shawna Robinson was 19 when she began racing—and not just cars. She drove everything from snowmobiles to monster trucks. She made her NASCAR debut in 1988. Through 2005, she had started 61 Busch races, three Truck races, and eight Cup races, including the 2002 Daytona 500.

Racing trucks? That's right, the Craftsman Series races specially built pickup trucks. That's Debbie Renshaw (above) powering to the lead in the No. 8 truck.

Debbie Renshaw was 10 years old in 1985, when she started hanging out at the racetrack with her dad, who was a racer.

"I loved fast cars and going fast even then," she says.

Debbie has been racing in NASCAR events since 2000. In 2005, she competed in all 25 races in the annual NASCAR Craftsman Truck Series. Her best finish was 12th. She's planning to race in 2006, too.

Racing Ahead

NASCAR has started a "Drive for **Diversity**" program to teach women, Hispanics, and African Americans to become stock car drivers and crew members. A total of 18 drivers, including five women, took part in the 2005 program.

Sarah Fisher had an outstanding IRL career before switching to stock cars in 2004. From 2000 to 2004, she started five Indy 500s. Sarah, who has been racing since she was 5, has been IRL's Most Popular Driver of the Year three times.

Sarah also does well in the classroom. After graduating with honors from high school, she attended college part-time while racing.

What's next for this racer girl? Sarah dreams of moving to the Nextel Cup series. "I want to be in anything with **fenders** on it," she said.

Here's a good look at the open-wheel Indy car driven by Sarah Fisher. The flaps at the front and back help the car handle more easily.

To get ready, Sarah ran 12 races in the 2005 Grand National West Series, a training ground for NASCAR.

3

OTHER KINDS OF Racing

Women compete in other types of auto racing besides IRL and NASCAR. Before Lyn St. James first drove in the Indy 500 in 1992, she raced in **endurance** races.

Lyn set 31 speed records during her incredible 20-year racing career. She finished 11th in that first Indy 500 and was the first woman named Rookie of the Year. Lyn started six more times at the Brickyard. Today, Lyn helps young women drivers who want to become successful racers.

OPPOSITE PAGE
Lyn St. James was 43 when she finally raced in the Indy 500 in 1992.

There are three kinds of drag racing: stock (cars that are like regular street cars); funny car (cars changed to look more like racers); and top fuel (long, skinny cars with huge engines). Dragsters are top fuel cars.

Drag races cover very short, straight distances and last only a few seconds. The specially built cars, called **dragsters**, can reach speeds of 330 miles (531 km) per hour on a quarter-mile (.4 km) track. At the end of the race, a parachute pops out of the car to slow it down.

Shirley "Cha Cha" Muldowney won three top fuel drag-racing world championships, in 1977, 1980, and 1982. She was the first man or woman to win more than one title.

Shirley won many races in her famous pink dragster. In 2003, she retired at age 63, after 30 years of drag racing. In 2004, she was elected to the International Motor Sports Hall of Fame.

With smoking tires and a roar from its powerful engine, Shirley's top fuel dragster "peels out" at the start of a race.

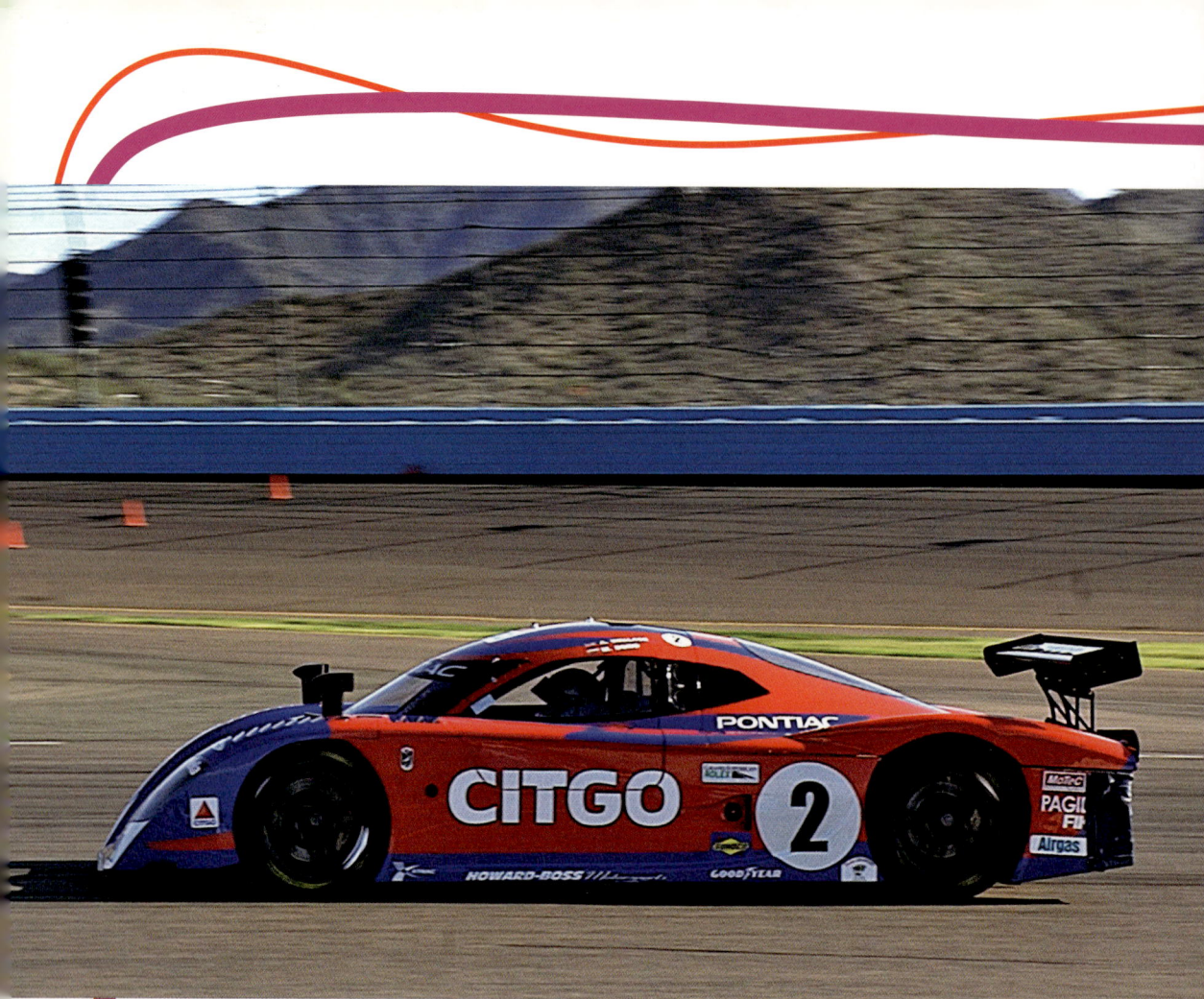

Venezuela's Milka Duno's busy life keeps her moving as fast off the track as she does on the track.

Sports car racing is another type of motor sport. Most sports cars are built as a mix between an open-wheel Indy racer and a NASCAR racer. Sports cars, though, have covered wheels.

Milka Duno is a top sports car driver. She was born in Venezuela and lives in Miami, Florida. In 2004, she became the first woman to win a race in the Rolex Sports Car Championship Series. Milka finished the 2005 season in eighth place.

Milka is a winner off the racetrack, too. She has four college degrees and has appeared on fashion magazine covers. She often speaks to groups of Hispanic children about the importance of education.

There are plenty of other fast-rising stars in auto racing. England's Katherine Legge is trying to become the first woman to drive in a Formula 1 race. Formula 1 is the top category of open-wheel racing and is very popular worldwide. Katherine won several races in similar types of series in 2005.

Next Dragster Star

Following in the footsteps of Shirley Muldowney is drag racer Hillary Will. After graduating from college, Hillary went to a special drag-racing school. At 25, she won the fifth race she ever entered.

Alison McLeod of Toronto, Canada, was just 16 in 2005 when she won a race in a midget car. Many drivers start with these small cars before moving up to bigger racers. Allison is now part of a program that helps young women racers.

The success of all the women in this book show that auto racing—of all types—is not just for men anymore!

Katherine Legge shows what all racers want to be: number one!

29

GLOSSARY

checkered flag a black-and-white checked flag that is waved as the winner of a race crosses the finish line

diversity in this case, the idea that society is made up of many different types of people

dragsters special motor vehicles built to go at very high speeds over short distances

endurance the ability to do something for a very long time—such as racing in endurance races over 12 hours long

fenders metal guards placed over the wheels of a car

laps trips around a racetrack (a lap is one trip)

media all the television and radio networks, newspapers, magazines, and Web sites that report news, and the people who work for them

NASCAR the National Association of Stock Car Auto Racing, the organizing group for most major stock car races

open-wheel a type of race car, such as Indy cars, on which the wheels aren't covered by fenders or the car's body

stock car a race car that looks like a regular passenger car but has a much more powerful engine and has many of the usual things removed

FIND OUT MORE

BOOKS

Danica Patrick: A Photo Tribute
(A.E. Engine, Minneapolis, MN) 2005
This book has tons of action and feature photos of today's most successful female race car driver.

Eyewitness NASCAR
by James Buckley, Jr. (DK Publishing, New York) 2005
A photo-filled book, it takes an inside look at America's most popular motor sport.

Lyn St. James
by Mark Stewart (Childrens Press, New York) 1996
This tells the story of one of the best female drivers of all time, including her runs in the famous Indy 500.

Women in Racing
by Michael Benson (Chelsea House, New York) 1997
Longer biographies of early woman pioneers in many forms of motor sports are told in this book.

WEB SITES

Visit our home page for lots of links about motor sports, women drivers, and different types of racing:
www.childsworld.com/links

Note to Parents, Teachers, and Librarians: We routinely check our Web links to make sure they're safe, active sites—so encourage your readers to check them out!

INDEX

Busch Grand National, 16, 17

car design, 7, 12, 21, 24, 26, 29

Christian, Sara, 14–15

Craftsman Truck Series, 16, 17, 18, 19

Daytona 500, 5, 17

drag racing, 24–25, 28

Duno, Milka, 26, 27

Fisher, Sarah, 20–21

Formula 1, 28

glossary, 30

go-karts, 6

Grand National West Series, 21

Guthrie, Janet, 5

Indianapolis 500, 4, 8, 9–10, 20, 23

Indy Racing League (IRL), 8, 11, 20

International Motor Sports Hall of Fame, 25

Legge, Katherine, 28

McLeod, Alison, 29

Moise, Patty, 17

Muldowney, Shirley "Cha Cha", 24–25

National Association for Stock Car Auto Racing (NASCAR), 5, 13–21

Nextel Cup, 16, 17

Patrick, Danica, 4–11

Renshaw, Debbie, 18–19

Robinson, Shawna, 16, 17

Rolex Sports Car Championship Series, 27

St. James, Lyn, 23

Smith, Louise, 15

sports car racing, 26–27

stock car racing, 12–21

truck racing, 16, 17, 18, 19

Will, Hillary, 28

BOB WOODS has written books for young readers as well as adults, with a special focus on motor sports such as NASCAR, motorcycles, and Formula 1 racing. He's also written about other sports, including baseball and basketball. He loves to ride motorcycles near his Connecticut home.

j 796.72 W861r
Woods, Bob.
Racer girls

CR